I0098636

Tomisms:
Random Thoughts on Everyday Life

By

Tom West

Wright Publishing Group, Inc.
St. Petersburg, FL 33715

ISBN: 978-0-69216904-9

Library of Congress Control Number: 2018909508

Names: West, Tom, 1952-
Title: Tomisms : random thoughts on everyday life / by Tom West.
Other Titles: Tom-isms! : random thoughts on everyday life
Description: St. Petersburg, FL : Wright Publishing Group, Inc., [2018]
Identifiers: ISBN 9780692169049
Subjects: LCSH: American wit and humor. | LCGFT: Anecdotes. | Humor.
Classification: LCC PS3623.E8469 T66 2018 | DDC 817/.6--dc23

Editing by Lisa A. Jimenez
Book design by Zack R. Mullikin

Printed and bound in the United States of America.

Published by
Wright Publishing Group, Inc.
1120 Pinellas Bayway South #205
St. Petersburg, FL 33715

Visit www.Tomisms.com for more information.

Foreword

Tom's favorite things (in no particular order): laughter, beer, friends, animals, bars, music, sports, island life, Tennessee Vols, family and love. That's what this book is about; his whacky take on what he sees in the things he enjoys – called Tomisms. He's the kind of guy you want sitting next to you at a bar, on an airplane or any get-together. He never intends to be the life of the party, but you know he is!

We appreciate you buying this book, and hope that it helps you make your best friend laugh so hard while reading one of Tom's random thoughts, they pee a little. Seriously, who knows -- one of these Tomisms could be the conversation starter you needed to make someone else laugh out loud and brighten his or her day? We need more of that!

This book is dedicated to all the friends, family and strangers who appreciate my sense of humor and join me in a good laugh each and every day. Special thanks to my publisher and friend, Lisa Wright-Jimenez, for her encouragement and expertise in making this book happen. As always, love and gratitude goes out to my wife Candee for enduring over 30 years of Tom-isms. I hope you enjoy this collection of laughs and will share it with someone you love.

About the Author

Tom West is a fun-loving entrepreneur, salesman and beer lover. For 25 years, he enjoyed working for a premier multi-national beer brewer before taking a brief hiatus to pursue a business in Costa Rica. Never venturing far from his friends and his love of beer, Tom returned to the industry and currently works for the one of the fastest-growing craft beer companies in America. Through it all, he found himself surrounded by creative and interesting people so he began jotting down observations, anecdotes and "Tom-isms" that altogether share his appreciation for the lighter side of life.

Table of Contents

CHAPTER 1: BEER, BUDDIES & BÄRWORTHY

Every loaf of bread is a tragic story of grains that could have become beer...but didn't.

I may not be able to walk the walk or talk the talk; but if you need somebody to drink the drink, then, I'm your man.

Gambling addiction hotlines would do so much better if every fifth caller were a winner.

Went on an alcohol diet while my friends were visiting. It worked; I lost three days!

Does beer go through your system so fast because it doesn't have to stop to change color?

24 hours in a day ... 24 beers in a case ...coincidence?

Botox could be considered a performance-enhancing drug for poker players.

Booze is the duct tape of life.

Remember that when someone annoys you, it takes 42 muscles in your face to frown, but it only takes 4 muscles to pick up your drink and ignore them.

I think maybe that Jack Daniels might be racist. I discovered last night that he doesn't get along with Jose Quervo at all!

Is baseball, the only field of endeavor where a man can succeed three times out of ten and be considered a star?

Sometimes when I reflect back on all the beer I drink, I feel ashamed. Then, I look into the glass and think about the workers in the brewery and all of their hopes and dreams. If I didn't drink this beer, they might be out of work and their dreams would be shattered. Then I say to myself, "It is better that I drink this beer and let their dreams come true than be selfish and worry about my liver."

AAA-AA: A club for people who are being driven to drink.

Women will never be equal to men until they can walk down the street with a baldhead and a beer gut, and still think they are sexy.

Proven fact: More people have died on treadmills than bar stools.

If life were fair, kegs would have wheels!

Childhood is like being drunk...everyone remembers what you did except you.

All I'm saying is I've noticed how tequila and good advice don't cross paths too often.

Tomisms

I was drinking at the bar, so I took a bus home. That may not be a big deal to you, but I've never driven a bus before.

I won't be impressed with technology until I can download beer!

My doctor told me to stop drinking and then told me to stop laughing!

If I saved all the money I spent on beer.... I'd spend it on beer!

Everyone has the "turning beer into pee" routine perfected. Now, who can figure out how to reverse the process?

I recently added squats to my workouts by moving the beer into the bottom shelf of the fridge.

The answer may not lie at the bottom of a bottle of beer but you should at least check.

Got a new password lock that takes a picture if anyone tries the wrong code to look in my phone. I now have 50 new close-up pictures of myself.

I am not self-medicating myself with beer. The guy at the beer store wrote me a prescription...well, he called it a receipt.... whatever.

Spilling a beer is the adult equivalent of losing a balloon.

Dinosaurs didn't drink beer and now they are extinct...coincidence? I think not.

Who's this "moderation" person everyone keeps telling me to drink with?

Online shopping is much more exciting if you drink too many margaritas and the unexpected packages start arriving a few days later.

Think what last call would look like if Wal-Mart had a bar.

A priest, a rabbi, and a pastor walk into a bar. The bartender looks up and says, "What is this, some kinda joke?"

"A beer, please."
"Sir, this is McDonalds."
"A McBeer, please."

I'm kind of glad dinosaurs are extinct because I'm pretty sure I would try to ride one after a few beers.

I used to see a life coach pretty frequently.... back when they were called bartenders.

If I'm ever on life support, unplug me.....then plug me back in.... see if that works.

Bad decisions make good stories.

Facebook needs a "I'll drink to that" button.

If I didn't drink, how would my friends know that I loved them at 2 am?

Tequila is Spanish for 'text your ex".

My idea of drinking responsibly is using a coaster.

Tomisms

We have a one-legged guy that works at the brewery. He's in charge of the hops.

Riddle: I have ten beers and someone asks me for one, how many beers do I have left? That's right...ten.

I've consumed truckloads of beer, barrels of gravy and partied like a rock star for years.... but now, I'm waiting one more hour to take an aspirin because of a warning label?

There's a fine line between genius and crazy. I like to use that line as a jump rope.

Why do people say it's hard to meet expenses when they're everywhere?

If one always takes life with a grain of salt --- shouldn't one, add a slice of lemon and a shot of tequila?

Aren't people who say they don't care what people think usually desperate to have people think they don't care what people think?

A fine beer may be judged with only one sip, but it's better to be thoroughly sure.

My bartender can beat up your therapist!

There would be a lot more Irish lawyers if they could just pass a bar.

The U.S. Is probably the only place in the world where people need energy drinks to sit in front of a computer all day.

One event they need in the World's Strongest Man Contest should be Pulling Apart Shopping Carts.

I really shouldn't have driven home from the bar last night. Especially since I walked there.

Went to a bar called Rick O'Sheas. Everybody was bouncing off the walls!

Tequila shots! Because it's Mexico somewhere!

If you don't drink, smoke or do drugs, you may live long enough to be a real burden to loved ones. Please get me some beer.

All my party planning skills revolve around exit strategies.

It takes a lot of balls to play golf the way I do.

My dentist told me to relax, then got all judgy about me drinking beer in his office. He needs to make up his mind.

Holiday drinking game: take a shot every time a relative says something rude.

I'm pretty sure that the last words I'm going to say before I kick the bucket will be...."How far do you think I can kick this bucket?"

Sober or not, if a cop ever asks me to recite the alphabet backward, I'm just going to put myself in the back of his car.

CHAPTER 2:
GETTING OLDER; STAY CURIOUS

How old would you be if you didn't know how old you are?

In the 60's, people took acid to make the world weird. Now, the world is weird and people take Prozac to make it normal.

You're never too old to toss random stuff in other people's shopping carts when they aren't looking.

Wouldn't you rather live life with an exclamation instead of an explanation?

Growing old is mandatory; growing up is optional.

If there were an Olympic Gold medal for making three trips upstairs before I got what I went for, my face would be on a box of Wheaties by now.

Do you find the older you get, the better you were?

If you die in an elevator, shouldn't you make sure to push the "up" button?

Is it a sign you are getting old when your houseplants are all alive, and you can't smoke any of them?

At what point do you stop lying about your age and start bragging about it?

Are you getting old when getting lucky means you found your car in the parking lot?

Are you pretty optimistic if you buy a burial suit with two pairs of pants?

Isn't getting old a very high price to pay for maturity?

Why do I act like I do? When I was a child, I saw Tarzan almost naked, Cinderella arrived home after midnight, Pinocchio told lies, Aladdin was a thief, Batman drove over 200 miles an hour, Snow White lived in a house with seven men, Popeye smoked a pipe and had tattoos, Pac Man ran around to digital music eating pills that enhanced his performance, and Shaggy and Snoopy were mystery-solving hippies that always had the munchies. I rest my case.

My biggest problem with the younger generation is I'm not in it.

Has anyone else thought of having a salt-rimmed casket?

I'm not inclined to resign to maturity!

Adulthood is like a visit to the vet; we're all excited about the ride until we realize where we're going.

Tomisms

A friend showed me a picture and said, "This was taken when I was younger." I said, "Every picture of you is when you were younger."

I remember when yoga was called Twister.

I can still remember a time when I knew more than my phone.

I may have only been young once, but I can be immature for a lifetime.

Intelligence is like underwear. It is important that you have it, but not necessary that you show it off.

You know you're getting older when your friends start having kids on purpose.

The first 60 years of childhood are always the hardest.

I'm not saying I've been around a while but when I was a kid, rainbows were black and white.

Isn't the best way to get a man to do something is to suggest he is too old for it?

The older I get, the earlier it gets late.

The best thing about the "good old days" is that I wasn't good and I wasn't old.

Back in my day, people used to take photos that had other people in them.

I guess the best thing about turning 100 years old is that there is no peer pressure.

If pro and con are opposites, wouldn't the opposite of progress be congress?

Do infants enjoy infancy as much as adults enjoy adultery?

How is it possible to have a "civil" war?

Why do fat chance and slim chance mean the same thing?

Why are there flotation devices under plane seats instead of parachutes?

Why do people tell you when they are speechless?

Have you ever imagined a world with no hypothetical situations?

Why do they call it an asteroid when it's outside the hemisphere, but call it a hemorrhoid when it's in your butt?

Why is it called plagiarism when you steal ideas from one person but to steal from many is research?

Why do they start the evening news with 'Good evening', and then proceed to tell you why it isn't?

If four out of five people suffer from diarrhea...does that mean that one enjoys it?

Do illiterate people get the full effect of Alphabet soup?

Why do they use sterilized needles for death by lethal injection?

Why do we put suits in a garment bag and put garments in a suitcase?

Tomisms

Why do banks leave the door wide open but the pens chained to the counter?

Where does the "o" come from when we abbreviate "number"?

Is it just me or doesn't anyone disappear in the Bermuda Triangle these days?

Isn't it easier to stay out then to get out?

How does a rumor without a leg to stand on get around some other way?

Why is it when we do something right, it gratifies some people and astonishes the rest?

Is dancing a perpendicular expression of a horizontal desire?

I'm against picketing but I don't know how to show it.

What is the opposite of medium?

Isn't the difference between stupidity and genius is that genius has its limits?

Isn't procrastination just the art of keeping up with yesterday?

Some people cause happiness wherever they go. Don't most people, however, cause happiness whenever they go?

I used to be indecisive. Should I have been?

Shouldn't we worry more about the unguided missiles?

What is an occasional table the rest of the time?

Should you take life seriously if nobody gets out alive anyway?

Is karaoke the Japanese term for tone deaf?

Isn't the remote control modern society's secular rosary?

Is Florida shaped like a handgun on purpose?

Isn't immigration the sincerest form of flattery?

Why is it "a word to the wise" when it's the stupid ones that need the advice?

Isn't the severity of the itch proportional to the extent of your reach?

Why will people pay more to be entertained than educated?

Hasn't income tax made more liars out of Americans than golf?

Do you sometimes feel like a fugitive from the law of averages?

Anyone else see the irony of a kidney-shaped swimming pool?

"I'm sorry" and "my bad" mean the same thing... unless you're at a funeral.

Isn't the real problem with jogging is that the ice keeps falling out of your glass?

If life were fair, wouldn't Elvis be alive and all the impersonators be dead?

Tomisms

I feel like I'm diagonally parked in a parallel universe.

If laughter really is the best medicine, then how come there are no doctors prescribing nitrous oxide?

Have you ever noticed that all the instruments searching for intelligent life are pointed away from Earth?

Doesn't your perception of how long a minute is depend on what side of the bathroom door you're on?

Why do towels get dirty if we only use them after washing ourselves?

Why do we always say "Heavens, No" but "Hell, Yeah"?

Can a hearse carrying a corpse drive in the carpool lane?

Why are they called stairs inside but steps outside?

You can be overwhelmed and underwhelmed, but why can't you be simply whelmed?

Don't too many people spend money they haven't earned, to buy things they don't want, to impress people they don't like?

Is talk cheap because supply exceeds demand?

If space is a vacuum, who changes the bags?

Is a clear conscience basically just a sign of a bad memory?
Is it true that for every action, there is an equal and opposite criticism?

Is the reason lightning doesn't strike twice in the same place is that the same place isn't there the second time?

You shouldn't sweat the petty things but should you pet the sweaty things?

Doesn't cleanliness become more important when godliness is unlikely?

So, technically, all shoes are buy one get one free.

Aren't those signs that say "Slow Children Playing" just mean?

If you are choking on an ice cube, couldn't you just wait it out?

Why isn't common sense more common?

Isn't cleaning just putting things in less obvious places?

Anybody else notice that people always try to do the right thing -- after they've tried everything else?

I grew up living paycheck to paycheck, but through hard work and perseverance, I now live direct deposit to direct deposit.

CHAPTER 4: LAUGH A LITTLE MORE

Can we just have a moment of silence for those who are currently sitting in traffic, on the way to the gym to ride a stationary bicycle?

Why can so few people hold their tongue when it weighs practically nothing?

Why do you have to "put your two cents in"... but it's only a "penny for your thoughts"? Where's that extra penny going?

Why are builders afraid to have a 13th floor but book publishers aren't afraid to have a Chapter 11?

Do you think the person who coined the phrase "slept like a baby" ever had one?

Why is it that when you're driving and looking for an address, you turn down the volume on the radio?

Is it true, times are so tough, that a picture is now only worth 200 words?

I bet the people who named "erectile dysfunction" was mad that "bone loss" was already taken.

Instead of candy, wouldn't it be easier to take, say, cabbage from a baby?

Wouldn't you behave better if there weren't so many options?

We have enough youth, how about a fountain of smart?

I will be posting telepathically today, so if you think of something funny.... that was me.

Doesn't the gene pool need a little more chlorine?

I saw a woman wearing a shirt with "Guess" on it...so, I said "implants?"

I saw that show *50 Things To Do Before You Die*, and I would have thought the obvious one was "shout for help."

I need a 7-second delay between my brain and my mouth. Well, maybe 15 seconds...ok, minutes.

I'm pretty sure my prayers are going to somebody's spam folder.

I would feel a lot safer if the drive-thru ATMs with Braille were located on the passenger side.

Don't worry about walking a mile in my shoes; just try spending a day inside my head.

It takes patience to listen; it takes skill to pretend you're listening.

Dance like no one is watching, because they're not; they're all checking their phones.

"Don't kid yourself" would be a great slogan for a condom company.

Why do they put pictures of criminals up in the post office? What are we supposed to do, write to them?

Is it rude to toss a Xanax in someone's mouth while they are talking?

"Because it would be hilarious" is probably not a good reason to elect someone to be president.

Having a garage sale! Come on by...my crap can be your crap!

Smartphones are pacifiers for adults.

Sometimes I spend entire meetings wondering how they got the big meeting table through the door.

So, we don't listen to scientists when they warn us about global warming but we'll listen to a rodent about the upcoming weather?

Who decided that we should sit together in groups while we chew food?

Whenever I have a headache, I take two aspirins and keep away from children, just like the bottle says.

Lazy is such an ugly word. I prefer "selective participation".

My swear jar could finance the space program.

Every time you make a typo....The errorists win.

I might have been driving a little crazy yesterday.... Siri came on and said, "In 400 feet, pull over and let me out."

I hope my "special place in hell" has beanbag chairs.

When asked what I did over the weekend...I reply, "Why, what did you hear?"

Studies show: 14,000 people are having sex right now; 25,000 people are kissing; 50,000 people are hugging; and you... Well, you're reading this.

My tolerance for idiots is extremely low today. I used to have some immunity built up, but obviously there's a new strain out.

I think I may need professional help....a chef, a butler and a maid should do it.

Someone's therapist knows all about me.

I guess my writing that "I give it 6 months" in the wedding guest book wasn't what they were looking for.

Florida...where the weather is so messed up, we give it names and then track it like a paparazzi stalks a celebrity in rehab.

It's Friday.... time to go make stories for Monday!

Whenever you feel worthless, remember, you were once the fastest sperm cell.

Mozart wrote his first symphony at the age of eight. I'm an adult and just rehearsed what I'm going to say at the drive-thru five times.

I gotta get my life together; this damn heat has made me realize I can't go to hell.

I think I've seized the wrong day!

Sometimes I just want to go where all the missing socks go.

My Facebook posts vacillate between really stupid and something that would prove I know what vacillate means.

There's no gangsta way to get out of a hammock.

Your shadow is a confirmation that light has traveled nearly 93 million miles unobstructed, only to be deprived of reaching the ground in the final few feet, thanks to you.

I was laughing way too hard to get mad when the guy with the 'coexist' bumper sticker flipped me off today.

I've never met a situation I couldn't avoid.

Some days you wake up and know it's the perfect day to be a bad example.

I just got 30 minutes of cardio trying to pick up an ice cube off of the kitchen floor.

It's called a "remote" because those are your odds of finding it when you want to change the channel.

Honesty is the best policy..................unless you want people to like you.

If you nap a lot, you significantly increase your chances of dying peacefully in your sleep.

Can we start the weekend over again? I wasn't ready.

When I die, I'm leaving my body to science fiction.

You say 4-hour car ride.... I say 4-hour live concert featuring me.

A mosquito landed on my friend's face...easiest decision of my life.

What the hell is a dew point and why do I need to know its number?

How many times are they going to make *Planet of the Apes*? Surely, another species has a planet that's worthy of a movie.

Never, ever, under any circumstances, take a sleeping pill and a laxative on the same night.

Wal-Mart needs an observation deck.

Any room is a panic room if you've lost your phone in it.

CHAPTER 5: REALITY & REALISMS

OK, who stopped payment on my reality check?

The fact that there is a highway to hell and only a stairway to heaven says a lot about anticipated traffic numbers.

Kinda wish I'd known my road to success was a toll road.

I should run for public office just to see what kind of scandalous dirt they dig up. I would love to piece together my 20's and 30's.

There's a fine line between genius and crazy. I like to use that line as a jump rope.

Isn't the real trouble with reality is that there's no background music?

If ignorance is bliss, why aren't there more happy people?

Why is physical courage so common in the world and moral courage so rare?

There are 249 millionaires in Congress. Now who said crime doesn't pay?

Life is a circus and I'm stuck in the freak tent!

Sometimes bad things happen to good people. I usually try to take photos when they do.

Not one shred of evidence supports the notion that life is serious.

I talk to people sometimes and think... Really? That's the sperm that won?

Did you ever notice thos: "the IRS" spells "theirs"?

I won't take a bullet for anyone because if I have time to jump in front of a bullet, you have time to move.

Scientists say that the universe is made up of neutrons, protons and electrons...they forgot to mention morons!

I look both ways before crossing a one-way street. That's how little faith I have left in humanity.

Having nutrition information on a bag of Cheetos is like having dating tips on a pair of Crocs.

Some people remind me of old TV sets: you have to hit them a couple of times for them to get the picture.

What if Netflix doubled as a dating service? "Here are seven other single people who watched *Grey's Anatomy* for eight hours straight last night."

Tomisms

Time may be a great healer but it's a crappy beautician.

Fifty Shades of Grey is only romantic because the guy's a billionaire. If he were living in a trailer, it would be a *Criminal Minds* episode.

There are only three things that tell the truth: small children, drunks and yoga pants.

Aren't interventions just judgmental surprise parties?

Don't you wish real life conversations had a 140-character limit?

My background check bounced!

If I've learned anything in life, it's that not enough people are at a loss for words.

Let's face it.... after Monday and Tuesday, even the calendar says W T F.

How come "you're a peach" is a compliment but "you're bananas" is an insult? Why are we allowing fruit discrimination to tear our society apart?

Remember when Sarah Palin was the craziest person in politics? Good times.

There were 16-year-olds competing at the Olympics and I still push on pull doors.

If I were two-faced, would I be wearing this one?

It is only when a mosquito lands on your testicles that you realize that there is always a way to solve problems without using violence.

At least my flip-flops fit every year.

Dance.... like no one is watching. Text and email...like it will be read in court one day.

I was having trouble with my computer, in a restaurant, and this young kid said he could help. He fixed it and I asked him what it was. He said it was an "id 10 t" issue. I asked him what that was and he said write it down, so I did: ID10T.

Whenever you're having a bad day, think of the guy who has to put the circus tent back in its bag.

Unfortunately, there is no dumbass vaccine!

Sometimes I meet people and feel bad for their dog.

Light travels faster than sound. Is that why some people appear bright until you hear them speak?

Can ghosts make babies with those hollow weenies?

Even if you are on the right track, won't you still get run over if you just sit there?

Do you think maybe that Earth is the insane asylum for the universe?

Why do people who know the least know it the loudest?

Is cremation thinking outside the box?

Isn't smoking one of the leading causes of statistics?

Tomisms

Anyone else know people who are potholes in the road to cheerful living?

I asked my North Korean friend how everything was over there. He said he couldn't complain.

Day 7 of drinking 96 ounces of water a day. A lot has changed. I pee 14 times a day; my skin feels great and I feel energized! I can now shapeshift into a lizard.

Instead of "hillbillies", shouldn't Tennesseans, under the new political correctness wave, be referred to as Appalachian-Americans?

Should we have to limit our madness to March?

I don't understand interventions. What's the point of being told I drink too much by a room full of reasons why I drink in the first place?

Forgive and forget, but shouldn't you keep a list of names just in case?

I live somewhere between playing my cards right and not playing with a full deck.

I like watching people try and figure out how much of a problem I'm going to be.

What does it mean if holy water sizzles when it hits your skin? Asking for a friend.

If I was a plastic surgeon.......I would 100% put a squeaky toy in every breast implant.

Wouldn't the worst time to have a heart attack be during a game of charades?

A real smart TV would increase the volume when you started eating chips.

I wonder if someone in the future will discover the ruins of Disneyland and think it's a temple of some bizarre mouse-worshipping cult?

Why does someone believe you when you say there are four billion stars, but check when you say the paint is wet?

When young people tell me about their problems, I like to tell them the story about that time I survived without my cell phone or the Internet.........for 40 years.

How is it that we put man on the moon before we figured out it would be a good idea to put wheels on luggage?

"Do not touch" must be scariest thing to read in Braille.

Being cremated is my last hope for a hot, smoking body.

I'm going to have to get rid of my memory foam mattress...it knows too much.

CHAPTER 6: SUPER POWERS & SUPER PEOPLE

I think I figured out Victoria's Secret. She's hungry.

Why does Superman stop bullets with his chest but ducks when you throw a revolver at him?

Why doesn't Tarzan have a beard?

If the professor on *Gilligan's Island* can make a radio out of a coconut, why can't he fix a hole in a boat?

Why is he the Lone Ranger when he always has Tonto with him?

If you choke a Smurf, what color will it turn?

Would Einstein be insulted if you offered him a penny for his thoughts?

Shouldn't Ronald McDonald be, like, heavier?

Mr. Rogers did not adequately prepare me for the people in my neighborhood.

Do you think Houdini ever locked his keys in his car?

Anyone else suddenly learn Kung Fu when you walk through a spider web?

Even Popeye didn't eat his spinach until he absolutely had to.

If Hooters delivered, would they be called Knockers?

The movie *Lincoln* did quite well in theaters. Pretty ironic if you think about it.

My boss told me, "Dress for the job you want; not the job you have". So now, I'm sitting in a disciplinary meeting dressed as Batman.

My definition of an intellectual is someone who can listen to the William Tell Overture without thinking of the Lone Ranger.

If you drive by a place with a guy dressed as the Statue of Liberty, waving at you, you have to know this place will prepare your taxes competently!

If I was a Jedi, there's a 100% chance I would use the "force" inappropriately.

Dear McDonalds...thank you for not serving hot dogs. I don't think I could order a super-sized McWeiner with a straight face.

Don't annoy me this month or I will give your phone number to every kid I see and tell them it's Santa's Hotline.

I'm not saying I'm Superman; we've just never been seen in the same room together.

ESPN Magazine is about to release its annual "Body Issue" which features 21 athletes posing nude. Along with the same promise as always: no bowlers.

Richard Branson has announced plans to develop a new type of plane that can fly from New York to Tokyo in one hour. Apparently, the engines are powered by human screams.

I wouldn't call it a superpower, but I have the ability to form an opinion and then keep it to myself.

If Superman was so smart, why were his underpants on the outside?

When Cheech and Chong split up, I wonder if they had to fight for joint custody.

The world's biggest problem was that Ross and Rachel were on a break. Can we go back to that time please?

Is Pee Wee Herman the only actor left who kept his hands to himself?

What's the point of making people like Paul McCartney and Elton John knights if they're not going to joust?

Why don't they just get Jehovah's Witnesses to deliver the mail?

Superman could have become a doctor, using his x-ray vision to detect life-threatening tumors. But no..... we really needed another journalist.

WARNING....COYOTE ACTIVITY:
Please call Animal Control if you observe any dangerous coyote activities:
• Carrying a box labeled ACME
• Dropping Anvil from hot air balloons
• In possession of catapult
• Detonating TNT
• Launching self with giant crossbow

On *Gilligan's Island*, how did Ginger have so many different outfits when they were only going on a 3-hour tour?

"The most difficult thing with quotes on the Internet is verifying them." – Abraham Lincoln

I'm not saying it's been raining, but I saw Noah at Home Depot.

Can a magician become disillusioned?

If Wyle E. Coyote had enough money to buy all that ACME crap, why didn't he just buy dinner?

Why do we choose from two people for president and fifty for Miss America?

Are people who are afraid of Santa Claus called claustrophobic?

Do you think it's a good idea to do card tricks for people you play poker with?

Trail mix is just M&Ms with obstacles.

If I had a militia, we wouldn't occupy a federal building, we would occupy a Krispy Kreme.

If Jimmy cracks corn and no one cares, why is there a song about him?

Who was the first person to look at a cow and ponder: "I think I'll squeeze these dangly things and drink whatever comes out?"

Why do croutons come in airtight packages? Aren't they just stale bread to begin with?

What disease did cured ham actually have?

If a parsley farmer is sued, can they garnish his wages?

What was the best thing before sliced bread?

Why is lemon juice made with artificial flavor and dishwashing liquid made with real lemons?

Why do people constantly return to the refrigerator with hopes that something new to eat will have materialized?

I shot my first turkey today. Scared the crap out of everyone in the frozen food section.

I just ordered a chicken and an egg off the Internet to see which one comes first. I'll keep you posted.

Some drink at the fountain of knowledge; others just gargle.

French toast is just regular toast that smokes cigarettes and has a tiny mustache.

Is it true that cannibals don't eat clowns because they taste funny?

Why does mineral water that has "trickled through mountains for centuries" go out-of-date next year?

I hate it when I think I'm buying organic vegetables and get home and discover they are just regular donuts.

I'm dieting for my chalk outline.

Saw some idiot at the gym put a water bottle where the Pringles can goes on the treadmill yesterday.

Is anyone else about three hamburgers away from being a vegan?

The makers of the 5-hour energy drink need to start making a 5-hour nap drink.

I read recipes the same way I read science fiction. I get to the end and I think, "Well, that's not going to happen."

I grew up under the threat of nuclear war...forgive me, if I can't muster up the appropriate terror at the prospect of gluten in my sandwich.

When I see a rich, snobby woman at the grocery store, I ask them, "Excuse me, do you work here?" Kinda keeps things real.

I've been eating Thin Mints for years...how long before I start seeing results?

Should vegetarians eat animal crackers?

I prefer my kale with a silent k.

I'm new to this whole baking thing. Tell me again.............how much whiskey goes into cookies?

I'm on a diet and nearly cut my finger off slicing up a salad. This never happens with cupcakes.

I read this article that said typical symptoms of stress are eating too much, impulse buying and driving too fast. Are you kidding? That's my idea of a perfect day!

Pilates? Oh, hell no!
I thought you said pie and lattes.

Raisin cookies that look like chocolate chip cookies are one of the reasons I have trust issues.

I don't sugarcoat my words.... I beer batter them.

I don't want to hear another word about "Obesity in America" until someone explains to me why a salad is $7 and a hamburger is a $1.

My secret ingredient is letting someone else cook.

If corn oil is made from corn, and vegetable oil is made from vegetables, what is baby oil made from?

Where in the nursery rhyme does it say Humpty Dumpty is an egg?

Don't you love people that order double cheeseburgers and large fries - with a diet coke?

What makes cheese so confidential that we actually need cheese shredders?

Here, all my life, I thought air was free until I bought a new bag of potato chips.

Even my fortune cookies just roll their eyes at me now.

If a cow laughed, would milk come out of its nose?

I saw a guy today at Starbucks: he had no smartphone, tablet or laptop. He just sat there drinking his coffee; like a psychopath.

One of the benefits of eating healthier is you never have to ask questions like, "Who ate my kale?"

Threw some protein bars in the trash and now a raccoon is bench-pressing the neighbor's Great Dane in the backyard.

Tomisms

Here's an idea: what about a smoke detector that will shut off when you yell, "I'm just cooking"?

Today's soup: whiskey with ice croutons.

I'm trying to lose just enough weight so that my hand fits comfortably in a Pringles can.

Are you trying to tell me a chicken fried this rice?

Yesterday was National Rum Day. Exercise makes you look better naked. So does rum. Your choice.

I burn about 2,000 calories every time I put on fitted sheets.

A new study finds that people who take their coffee black are more likely to exhibit psychopathic tendencies. People who order a quad shot, non-fat, vanilla soy, extra foam, light whip with caramel drizzle, are more likely to be the victims.

What came first: the fruit or the color orange?

Who was the first person to say, "See that chicken? I'm going eat the next thing that comes outta its butt"?

When life gives you lemons, shouldn't you cut them in half and squirt life in the eye?

I'm glad I don't have to hunt for my food; I don't even know where sandwiches live.

What do chickens think we taste like?

When dog food has a new and improved taste, who tests it?

Aren't families like fudge -- mostly sweet with a few nuts?

Isn't coffee just to keep you going until it's acceptable to drink wine?

When I was a kid, we had to eat Tide right out of the box.

The good thing about iced tea is that you can drink it at work. The good thing about Jack Daniels is that it looks like iced tea.

Ever notice that the roof of your car is the worst cup holder ever?

I'm going to open a restaurant named "Peace & Quiet" where kids' meals are $250.

When the hostess at the restaurant says, "Table for two?" I like to act surprised and say, "You can see her too?"

So, what do they plant to get seedless watermelons?

I put Red Bull in my Hummingbird feeder...I'm pretty sure I just saw one go back in time.

As a child, was your family's menu like mine: two choices, take it or leave it?

A new study shows that LSD will help you lose weight. That make sense cause it's kind of hard to get to the fridge with a dragon guarding it.

Of all the possible utensils that could have been invented to eat rice with, how did two sticks win out?

Isn't pizza all about geometry? A circle made of triangles inside a square box.

Why does Sea World have a seafood restaurant? Are you eating a slow learner?

CHAPTER 8:
WIVES, WOMEN & WHAT I WANT TO KNOW

Best relationship advice: Make sure you're the crazy one.

Relationships are like algebra...ever looked at your X and wonder Y?

Women talk about makeup like it's a weapon:
"What kind of eye shadow is that?"
"Oh, it's the Mac 34XZ10 Pro Supreme Blend 10 points to Gryffindor".

Women are smarter than men, but men have the advantage of not knowing this.

"I am" is reportedly the shortest sentence in the English language. Could it be that "I do" is the longest sentence?

Is the reason the average woman would rather have beauty than brains is because the average man can see better than he can think?

My wife nominated me for the ice bucket challenge. I'm a little confused; has anyone else been asked to hold a toaster at the same time?

Aren't women like phones? They love to be held, loved to be talked too, but if you press the wrong button, won't they love to disconnect you?

I love being married. Isn't it great to find that one special person you can annoy for the rest of your life?

A woman always gets the last word in an argument: so, would the next word be the start of a new argument?

Isn't the real reason women don't play football is because eleven of them would never wear the same outfit in public?

Wouldn't relationships be easier if people came with a "clear history" button?

Aren't relationships a two-way street navigated by women who are backseat drivers and men who refuse to use maps?

I don't think I'd be too good in a threesome: I can't even pet two dogs at the same time!

Most people want a perfect relationship...I just want a hamburger that looks like the ones in commercials.

And God promised man that good and obedient wives would be found in all corners of the world, and then he made the Earth round...and just laughed and laughed and laughed.

Tomisms

My wife is only a couple of apps away from never having to speak to me again.

My wife and I were sitting on the couch when she says, "I love you." I said, "Is that you or the wine talking?" and she said, "I was talking to the wine!"

Why isn't their an app that when your girlfriend/ wife really needed to talk to you during the game, she would appear in a little box in the corner of the screen during a time-out?

First, my wife tells me to be myself and then she's telling me to stop being an idiot. She's got to make her mind up!

So , my friend was bouncing around channels and was going back and forth from the porn channel and the fishing channel. His wife finally said, "Honey, just stay on the porn channel, you already know how to fish".

Every time I see a beautiful woman with a goofball, I think to myself...this is a pretty good picture of us.

A recent study has found that women who carry a little extra weight live longer than the men who mention it.

Never marry a woman who was captain of the debate team.

You're never childless when you have a husband.

If love is blind, why is lingerie so popular?

Behind every great man is a woman rolling her eyes.

My wife says she lives with the perfect man. Unfortunately, she meant Mr. Coffee.

If a man is walking in a forest and no woman is there to hear him, is he still wrong?

Just read that 4,153,237 people got married last year, not to cause any trouble but shouldn't that be an even number?

I'm living proof that my wife can take a joke.

I was struggling with my bucket list, then I changed the B to an F and now I'm good to go.

Never ask a woman who's eating ice cream right out of the carton how she's doing!

Women love cats. Cats are independent, they don't listen, they don't come in when you call, they like to stay out all night, and when they're home they like to be left alone and sleep. Aren't these the very qualities that women hate in men?

My wife and I had words last night, but I didn't get to use any of mine!

Why does a woman work ten years to change a man's habits and then complain that he's not the man she married?

Women: you should quit dating sites and start concentrating on pizza delivery guys; before you even meet them, you know they have a job, a car and..... pizza!

I only do what the voices in my wife's head tell her to tell me to do.

If at first you don't succeed, shouldn't you try doing it like your wife told you to do it?

I asked my wife "Hey honey, what did you change the Wi-Fi password to?" She responded with "our anniversary date" --- she did this on purpose.

Do man-eating sharks just not like the taste of women?

I hate it when my wife accuses me of something I didn't think she knew about.

I might drive my wife crazy, but at least it'll be the scenic route.

"Engagement" can mean either planning to marry or initiating combat. Coincidence?

I know what women want. They want you to drag them into the bedroom, throw them on the bed and do the dishes while they take a nap.

Sex burns 360 calories per hour. Why do they measure it by the hour?

Why are his-and-her presents always for her?

Hurricane season! Aren't hurricanes like women: when they come, they're wet and wild, but when they leave they take your house and car?

When you walk into a singles bar shouldn't you remember your Mom's wise words? "Don't pick that up, you don't know where it's been!"

Isn't Romeo & Juliet the perfect example of why communication within a relationship is so crucial?

Is it true that the only reason they say 'Women and children first' is to test the strength of the lifeboats?

My dentist told me I need a crown. I was like... I know, right?

My core workout comes from being around women and sucking in my gut.

Osama Bin Laden was living with three wives in one compound and never left the house for five years. Is it true that he called the Navy Seals himself?

Women spend more time wondering what men are thinking then men spends actually thinking.

If I got $1 every time a woman said I wasn't her type, I'd be her type.

My wife asked me what I wanted from Santa...I guess "to tell me where the naughty girls are" wasn't the right answer.

I remember when safe sex was a padded headboard.

Sometimes isn't the best kind of birth control just good lighting?

Whoever said, "your harshest critic is yourself" was clearly never married.

It's crazy that your brain can calculate where to put your hand to catch a 90-mph fastball, but won't keep your mouth shut when a woman is angry.

Tomisms

Men read *Playboy* for the articles; women go to malls for the music.

What should you give a man who has everything? A woman to show him how to work it all.

When Miley Cyrus is naked and licks a hammer, it's considered "art"...when I do it, I'm "drunk" and have to leave Home Depot.

When a woman wears leather clothing, a man's heart beats faster, his throat gets dry, his knees get weak, and he begins to act irrationally. Ever wonder why? She smells like a new truck.

Ninety percent of being married is shouting "what" from different rooms.

I don't understand why Cupid was chosen to represent Valentine's Day. When I think of romance, the last thing that comes to my mind is a short, chubby toddler coming at me with a weapon.

There are only three kinds of men who don't understand women: young men, old men, and middle-aged men.

Is it politics or marriage that makes strange bedfellows?

When people say "we're expecting a baby" does that mean there could be other outcomes?

Do you think other dogs think Poodles are members of a weird religious cult?

After someone gets married, is his wallet full of pictures of her, where his money used to be?

Isn't a marriage certificate just another name for a work permit?

Every time you talk to your wife, your mind should remember that: "This conversation will be recorded for training and quality purposes."

Nothing says I love you more than a tracking device.

My wife told me nothing shocks her anymore so I switched her digital scale from lbs. to kg.

Someone asked me what my wife spends on a bottle of wine....
I told them maybe a half an hour...more or less.

I asked the trainer at my gym, "Which machine should I use to impress women? And he said "the ATM."

There's no doubt in my mind women should rule the world...there would be no wars, just a bunch of jealous countries not talking to each other.

My wife seems to think I'm like that one crazy wheel on a grocery cart.

If your man is reluctant to talk about his feelings, it's probably because you haven't told him what they are yet.

My buddy is getting a divorce. They split the house...he got the outside.

A new study shows that marriage is more beneficial to men than women. The results of this study were shouted at me through a locked bedroom door.

I am presently experiencing life at a rate of several WTFs per hour.

Doesn't the probability of meeting someone you know increases a hundredfold when you're with someone you're not supposed to be seen with?

All I ask is a chance to prove money can't make me happy.

Tomisms

When a woman says "what?", is it because she didn't hear you or is she giving you a chance to change what you said?

Isn't the Wizard Of Oz the ultimate chick flick, two women trying to kill each other over shoes?

Got outvoted 1-1 by my wife again.

I could survive three months in the wilderness with a pocketknife and the contents of a woman's purse.

My wife told me she wanted the body of a stripper, but she raised hell when I brought her one.

Most household injuries are caused by saying "whatever" during an argument with your wife.

My wife says I never listen to her...or something like that.

Arguing with your wife is like reading the Software Licensing Agreement. In the end, you ignore everything and click..."I Agree"

Share the laughter; buy a copy of this book for a friend!

To purchase or for more information, please visit www.Tomisms.com.